This book is a

Gift

From

....

To

....

Date

....

May God bless you through this book

Prayers for a happy married life

PRAYERS FOR A HAPPY MARRIED LIFE

PRAYERS FOR A HAPPY MARRIED LIFE

Copyright © 2014

PRAYER M. MADUEKE

ISBN: **9781500183233**

Prayer Publications

First Edition, 2014

For further information of permission

1 Babatunde close, off Olaitan Street, Surulere, Lagos, Nigeria
+234 803 353 0599
Email: pastor@prayermadueke.com,
Website: www.prayermadueke.com

Dedication

This book is dedicated to people who are trusting God to experience fullness of joy and happiness in their marriage. The Lord who sees your sincere dedication will answer your prayers Amen.

Prayers for a happy married life

BOOK OVERVIEW

PRAYERS FOR A HAPPY MARRIED LIFE

- *The covenant of marriage*
- *How marriages come under attack*
- *Trust God to lead you to marry*
- *How God guides His children*

THE COVENANT OF MARRIAGE

While everyone desires to marry (or be married), few people really take their time to study and understand the true meaning of the covenant of marriage. It is highly important to understand the covenant of marriage before going into it so that you could be successful.

In this book, you will learn what it entails to make a good decision and how to know it is the will of God or not. Armed with this knowledge, you will get married and remain happy to the end. Many people rush into marriage without planning what they want to get out of it. Others know what they are supposed to get but do not know how to get them. Some depend on their partners and are ready to take anything from them. Because of this, many people have married whomever it was that came to marry them. Failing to find out what God has said or His plans for your marriage would make you to accept even what the devil or his agents offer you. The marriage institution started from the beginning, so no one has any excuse to fail.

> *"18And the LORD God said, it is not good that the man should be alone; I will make him a help meet for him. 19And out of the ground the LORD God formed every beast of the field and every fowl of the air; and brought them unto Adam to see what he would call them: and whatsoever Adam called every living creature that was the name thereof. 22And the rib, which the LORD God had taken from man, made he a woman, and brought her unto the man"* (Genesis 2:18-19, 22).

Marriage covenant is a lifetime covenant. In this particular covenant, God does not expect it to be

2

broken. Once this covenant is broken, every other covenant with God concerning your life is affected.

> *"Yet ye say, wherefore? Because the LORD hath been witness between thee and the wife of thy youth, against whom thou hast dealt treacherously: yet is she thy companion, and the wife of thy covenant. And did not he make one? Yet had he the residue of the spirit. In addition, wherefore one? That he might seek a godly seed. Therefore, take heed to your spirit, and let none deal treacherously against the wife of his youth. For the LORD, the God of Israel, saith that he hateth putting away: for* one *covereth violence with his garment, saith the LORD of hosts: therefore take heed to your spirit that ye deal not treacherously"* (Malachi 2:14-16).

God is a witness between any man and woman that enter into this covenant of marriage. God monitors every detail of the man's actions or the woman's actions towards each other. You cannot dissolve marriage once it is contracted and confirmed. God hates treacherous dealings in marriage. God commanded that a married couple should stay together the rest of their lives. Therefore, it is wrong to rush into marriage or be careless over the choice of your partner. Covenant is a very serious issue because if you break it ignorantly, you will definitely suffer for it.

> *"¹Then there was a famine in the days of David three years, year after year; and David enquired of the LORD. In addition, the LORD answered, it is for Saul, and for* his *bloody house, because he slew the Gibeonites. ²And the king called the Gibeonites, and said unto them; (now the Gibeonites* were *not of the children of Israel, but*

3

> *of the remnant of the Amorites; and the children of Israel had sworn unto them: and Saul sought to slay them in his zeal to the children of Israel and Judah.)* ³*Wherefore David said unto the Gibeonites, What should I do for you? In addition, wherewith shall I make the atonement that ye may bless the inheritance of the LORD?* ⁶*Let seven men of his sons be delivered unto us, and we will hang them up unto the LORD in Gibeah of Saul,* whom *the LORD did choose. In addition, the king said, I will give* them. ⁹*And he delivered them into the hands of the Gibeonites, and they hanged them in the hill before the LORD: and they fell* all *seven together, and were put to death in the days of harvest, in the first* days, *in the beginning of barley harvest"* (2 Samuel 21:1-3, 6, 9).

The reason many people are suffering today is because they broke a covenant or they are one with people that broke a covenant. A broken covenant affects children, born and those yet to be born.

> *"Remember, O LORD, what is come upon us: consider, and behold our reproach. Our inheritance is turned to strangers, our houses to aliens. We are orphans and fatherless, our mothers* are *as widows. We have drunken our water for money; our wood is sold unto us.* ⁵*Our necks* are *under persecution: we labor,* and *have no rest. We have given the hand* to *the Egyptians,* and to *the Assyrians, to be satisfied with bread"* (Lamentations 5:1-6).

It brings reproach and seizure of inheritance. It causes its victims to lose their blessings to strangers and aliens. It increases the number of orphans, widowers and widows in a place. Broken covenant is very destructive and leads people into bondage and captivity. The terrible part of it is that many victims of broken covenants are not aware of it. They suffer because of evil inheritance. It can reduce a greatly destined prince to a slave boy or house cleaner. Can you imagine someone who was destined to become a president cleaning the streets and begging for handouts? This is disaster.

> *"Our fathers have sinned,* and are *not; and we have borne their iniquities. Servants have ruled over us: there is none that doth deliver* us *out of their hand. We gat our bread with* the peril of *our lives because of the sword of the wilderness"* (Lamentations 5:7-9).

What you are going through now could be because of a broken covenant. If your father is a polygamous man, then you could be a victim of inherited evil covenant. That may be the reason why family or circumstances are pushing you to make a wrong choice of your partner. You need to study your foundation very well before you make a choice of whom to marry.

> *"The word of the LORD came also unto me, saying, Thou shall not take thee a wife, neither shall thou have sons or daughters in this place. For thus saith the LORD concerning the sons and concerning the daughters that are born in this place, and concerning their mothers that bare them, and concerning their fathers that begat them in this land; They shall die of grievous deaths; they shall not be lamented; neither shall they be buried; but they shall be as dung upon the face of the earth: and they shall be consumed by the sword, and by famine; and their carcasses shall be meat for the fowls of heaven, and for the beasts of the earth"* (Jeremiah 16:1-4).

5

You can correct other mistakes in other areas of life or put them away but not in the covenant of marriage. If you do so, it affects your relationship with God for God hates putting away of legal partners. Covenant is a legal contract that binds you and your partner for life on earth.

> *"But if ye bite and devour one another, take heed that ye be not consumed one of another"* (Galatians 5:15).

As soon as marriage is ordained, it becomes an unalterable and an irrevocable commitment. Breaking the covenant of marriage is not a mere thing because it can ruin a generation yet to be born. If you decide to separate from your partner and live apart, you would be tempted to sin. If you divorced and remarried, then you are living on earth committing adultery. It is contrary to the Word God.

> *"Without understanding, covenant breakers, without natural affection, implacable, unmerciful: Who knowing the judgment of God, that they which commit such things are worthy of death, not only do the same, but have pleasure in them that do them"* (Romans 1:31-32).

When you have limited understanding about marriage, you are likely to break this covenant. Once you break the covenant of marriage, it destroys your affection and your character. The emergence of hatred at home signals the failure of marriage. Other things that could break any marriage include having unforgiving spirit and being inconsiderate and unmerciful. At that point, if you do nothing, you will no longer regard the consequence of your actions that would attract God's judgment.

Soon you would begin to question certain principles that guide marriage, which you believed in earlier. You may even write, teach and preach to others to deviate from faith. But if you are keeper of a marriage covenant, you will always show mercy and forgiveness to your partner.

HOW MARRIAGES COME UNDER ATTACK

When couples begin to find faults among themselves, divorce spirit enters into their marriage. Whether your wife knows how to cook or not, you have no right to divorce her. You have been bound to remain with your husband even when he does not know how to dress his bed, dress very well or speak good grammar. He may not know how to make you happy or tell you he loves you but he is your lawful husband.

It is better not to marry at all than to marry and discover that your wife or husband is not the right person God has ordained for you. That is why you need to take time to confirm God's will before taking the marriage vow. God will not give you two women that are alive to marry or allow you to divorce and re-marry. It cannot be His will.

"The Pharisees also came unto him, tempting him, and saying unto him, is it lawful for a man to put away his wife for every cause? And he answered and said unto them, Have ye not read, that he which made them at the beginning made them male and female, And said, For this cause shall a man leave father and mother, and shall cleave to his wife: and they twain shall be one flesh? Wherefore they are no more twain, but one flesh. What therefore God hath joined, let not man put asunder. They say unto him, why did Moses then command to give a writing of divorcement, and to put her away? He saith unto them, Moses because of the hardness of your hearts suffered you to put away your wives: but from the beginning, it was not so. And I say unto you,

whosoever shall put away his wife, except it be for fornication, and shall marry another, committed adultery: and whoso married her who is put away doth commit adultery" (<u>Matthew 19:3-9</u>).

You are not permitted to kill your wife or husband in order to marry again because when you do, you become a murderer. I am talking to the single men and women, bachelors and unmarried women who have never married. Think very well, look very well, and pray very well before you make your final decision because the woman you are going to marry will remain with you for life. If she gives you the forbidden fruit, you still do not have the right to poison her or divorce her.

The reason why you should wait enough and make sure that God directs you is that many people are now suffering because they made wrong choices of marriage partner. There are husbands and wives that are living together but they do not discuss or plan together. They eat from the same plate but they are not one indeed. They are like two traders in the same shop that do not think alike.

A couple whose marriage is suffering attacks from devil must have failed to consider each other, comfort and admonish each other. They must have failed to submit to each other, prefer each other, forgive and bear each other's burden. They are not praying for themselves or greeting each other. Yet God has commanded them to do so, as a debt they owe each other (*See* <u>1 Thessalonians 4:18</u>; <u>Hebrews 10:24</u>; <u>Colossians 3:13</u>; <u>1 Peter 5:5</u>; <u>Romans 12:10</u>). When you love your partner truly, you would practice the above things daily with joy and gladness.

"Confess your *faults one to another, and pray one for another, that ye may be healed. The effectual fervent prayer of a righteous man availed much"* (James 5:16).

"Not forsaking the assembling of ourselves together, as the manner of some is; *but exhorting* one another: *and so much the more, as ye see the day approaching"* (Hebrews 10:25).

"Forbearing one another, and forgiving one another, if any man have a quarrel against any: even as Christ forgave you, so also do *ye"* (Colossians 3:13).

A husband and his wife should pray for each other and fellowship together because they are one before God. If you are not married yet, I want to believe that you will allow God to lead you to your angel. I pray your marriage would be likened to heaven on earth. When you trust God enough, you would notice that the best thing that could take place on earth after your salvation is a good marriage. Do not worry. Christian marriage is different from societal marriage or the marriage of backslidden believers. Trust God and He will crown your life with a godly spouse.

TRUST GOD TO LEAD YOU TO MARRY

Right from the beginning of time, God made the woman for the man. God's purpose for marriage is partnership, procreation, pleasure, protection, preservation of purity and provision. None of these things can be obtain elsewhere other than marriage.

> *"28And God blessed them, and God said unto them, Be fruitful, and multiply, and replenish the earth, and subdue it: and have dominion over the fish of the sea, and over the fowl of the air, and over every living thing that moved upon the earth. 18And the LORD God said,* It is *not good that the man should be alone; I will make him a help meet for him"* (Genesis 2:18; 1:28).

> *"Drink waters out of thine own cistern and running waters out of thine own well. Let thy fountains be dispersed abroad,* and *rivers of waters in the streets. Let them be only thine own, and not strangers' with thee. Let thy fountain be blessed: and rejoice with the wife of thy youth"* (Proverbs 5:15-18).

> *"Likewise, ye husbands, dwell with* them *according to knowledge, giving honor unto the wife, as unto the weaker vessel, and as being heirs together of the grace of life; that your prayers be not hindered"* (1 Peter 3:7).

> *"Nevertheless,* to avoid *fornication, let every man have his own wife, and let every woman have her own husband"* (1 Corinthians 7:2).

> *"But if any provide not for his own, and especially for those of his own house, he hath*

denied the faith, and is worse than an infidel" (1 Timothy 5:8).

Trust God and lean on Him for provisions so that He fulfills His purpose for your marriage in your lifetime. You need God's leading in this area no matter how wise you are because God is the only one capable of connecting you to the best partner. An unsaved person is blind to the future and ignorant of the consequences of today's decision about the future. The Scriptures puts it this way:

> *"There is a way that seemed right unto a man, but the end thereof* are *the ways of death"* (Proverbs 16:25).

> *"O LORD, I know that the way of man* is *not in himself:* it is *not in man that walked to direct his steps"* (Jeremiah 10:23).

> *"And it came to pass, when they were come, that he looked on Eliab, and said, Surely the LORD'S anointed* is *before him. But the LORD said unto Samuel, Look not on his countenance, or on the height of his stature; because I have refused him: for* the LORD *seeth not as man seeth; for man looked on the outward appearance, but the LORD looked on the heart"* (1 Samuel 16:6-7).

You may have succeeded in making good choices in other areas of your life but when it comes to marriage, you need to consult God from the beginning. Even a true child of God should not rush into any decision without God leading him.

Samuel would have made a terrible mistake in his choice of the first king of Israel. Everyone needs God at the point of making a choice of whom to marry or else there are bound to be mistakes as many couples are regretting today and wishing they never got married. Only God has the eyes to see what is good for you especially in the area of marriage. That is why you cannot do without God in the issue of marriage.

> "*16And I will bring the blind by a way* that *they knew not; I will lead them in paths* that *they have not known: I will make darkness light before them, and crooked things straight. These things will I do unto them, and not forsake them. 19Who is blind, but my servant? Or deaf, as my messenger* that *I sent? Who is blind as he that is perfect, and blind as the LORD'S servant? 20Seeing many things, but thou observes not; opening the ears, but he heareth not. 8Then shall thy light break forth as the morning, and thine health shall spring forth speedily: and thy righteousness shall go before thee; the glory of the LORD shall be thy rewarded*" (Isaiah 42:16, 19-20; 58:8).

When you ignore God while making a choice and then invite Him to see and approve your choice, you may not get His approval. No matter what you see and know about a person, your knowledge is limited (*See* Acts 10:9-20; 16:6-10; 2 Corinthians 3:5).

> "*For we are but of yesterday, and know nothing, because our days upon earth are a shadow*" (Job 8:9).

> "*Likewise the Spirit also helped our infirmities: for we know not what we should pray for as we ought: but the Spirit itself makes intercession for us with groaning which cannot be uttered. And he that searched the hearts knoweth what* is *the mind of the Spirit, because he makes intercession for the saints according to* the will of God. And

we know that all things work together for good to them that love God, to them who are the called according to his *purpose"* (<u>Romans 8:26-28</u>).

Do not desert God now that you are thinking of whom to marry. Otherwise, you may suffer terrible mistakes. Every believer needs God's guidance especially when making a choice of a marriage partner. God will be happy when you tell Him to help you choose a life partner. In this way, you would have involved Him. God is able to follow you all the way to make sure that you succeed.

The truth is that man cannot direct his ways or steps. However, many wise men have followed the paths they discovered for themselves without God only to find out that they have made great mistakes when it was too late. God does not want you to be a victim of such terrible mistakes. Therefore, commit your ways to Him and He shall cause you to prosper. To understand the will of God for your life, you must commit your ways unto God and follow Him patiently with prayers.

No man can boast of knowing tomorrow because only God knows tomorrow. Your decision of whom you married would be weighed in the future. Therefore, do not boast of limited things you see now. God knows everything about yesterday, today and tomorrow, even eternity. The money, cars and material things you are see now may no longer be available tomorrow. It would be a terrible mistake to put your trust in them.

Beauty is still available because slayers of beauty may be waiting for you to exhaust all your strength. On the other hand, do certificate and credentials provide all the confidence you need? Remember they are only ordinary papers. More so, there is the possibility of the brain malfunctioning tomorrow and all the papers and credentials would be useless and unprofitable. You do not have the capability to tell much about yourself, how much more another person. It is better to put your trust in the Lord and hope for the best.

There are credible information about you, which only God knows. God knows the woman or man that can stay with you at all cost and ones that will abandon you when you need them most. Do not choose your partner by sight because you may regret it later.

> *"For they that are after the flesh do mind the things of the flesh; but they that are after the Spirit the things of the Spirit. For to be carnally minded* is *death; but to be spiritually minded* is *life and peace. Because the carnal mind* is *enmity against God: for it is not subject to the law of God, neither indeed can be"* (Romans 8:5-7).

> *"[11]For what man knoweth the things of a man, save the spirit of man which is in him? Even so, the things of God knoweth no man, but the Spirit of God. [14]But the natural man receiveth not the things of the Spirit of God: for they are foolishness unto him: neither can he know* them, *because they are spiritually discerned"* (1 Corinthians 2:11, 14).

Only God can know the content of the human heart. Therefore, allow God to be your matchmaker, if you want to succeed in marriage. As you pray, close your eyes to receive and open it to see whom God has given to you. He promised to lead us even when we are blind. You need to say, "O Lord, is it Your will. Let Your will be done." Great people of God who failed to do allow the will of God for their marriages are regretting now.

"16And I will bring the blind by a way that they knew not; I will lead them in paths that they have not known: I will make darkness light before them, and crooked things straight. These things will I do unto them, and not forsake them. 19Who is blind, but my servant? Alternatively, deaf, as my messenger that I sent? Who is blind as he that is perfect, and blind as the LORD'S servant? 20Seeing many things, but thou observes not; opening the ears, but he heareth not" (Isaiah 42:16, 19-20).

It is better to allow God to show you your partner than to show God whom you have chosen to marry. God may not argue with you but if you come back to complain, He might as well not listen.

"22Whoso findeth a wife findeth a good thing, and obtained favor of the LORD. 14House and riches are the inheritance of fathers: and a prudent wife is from the LORD" (Proverbs 18:22; 19:14).

"For I know the thoughts that I think toward you, saith the LORD, thoughts of peace, and not of evil, to give you an expected end. Then shall ye call upon me, and ye shall go and pray unto me, and I will hearken unto you. And ye shall seek me, and find me, when ye shall search for me with all your heart" (Jeremiah 29:11-13).

God is omniscience, perfect and has never made any mistake. Therefore, you need to trust Him. The best testimony about marriage is to say, "The Lord gave my partner to me, and it is a great favor."

You can get houses and riches or inherit them from your earthly father, but only God gives a wife or husband. If you want a virtuous and prudent wife, go to the Lord. Even before you were born, God had ordained your spouse. So, do not rush out to do it on your own way. Ask God to lead you. His thoughts towards you are of peace and not of evil, to give you an expected end. He will be happy and well pleased if you cast your problems unto Him. If you ask and you do not find, seek Him with all your heart and He will grant you your heart desires.

> "*³Trust in the LORD, and do good; so shall thou dwell in the land, and verily thou shall be fed. ⁴Delight thyself also in the LORD; and he shall give thee the desires of thine heart. ⁵Commit thy way unto the LORD; trust also in him; and he shall bring it to pass. ²⁵I have been young, and now am old; yet have I not seen the righteous forsaken, nor his seed begging bread. ¹¹For the LORD God is a sun and shield: the LORD will give grace and glory: no good* thing *will he withhold from them that walk uprightly*" (Psalms 37:3-5, 25; 84:11).

God is eternal, all knowing and cannot be deceived. While physical appearances and empty promises can deceive you, they cannot deceive God. In fact, He has promised to guide us. So why would you not trust Him and get the best from Him? Trust in the Lord and remain faithful and committed to His Word. Commit all your ways unto Him now and depend on Him fully. His plans for you would make you happy today, tomorrow and forever. He will be a sun that would rise to lead your marriage and a shield to protect your marriage. Your marriage will never lack God's grace and glory when you allow God to lead you. Likewise, no good thing will lack in your marriage according to His Word.

"But Zion said, the LORD hath forsaken me, and my Lord have forgotten me. Can a woman forget her sucking child, that she should not have compassion on the son of her womb? Yea, they may forget, yet will I not forget thee" (Isaiah 49:14-15).

"22The light of the body is the eye: if therefore thine eye be single, thy whole body shall be full of light. 23But if thine eye were evil, thy whole body shall be full of darkness. If therefore the light that is in thee be darkness, how great is that darkness! 24No man can serve two masters: for either he will hate the one, and love the other; or else he will hold to the one, and despise the other. Ye cannot serve God and mammon. 25Therefore I say unto you, Take no thought for your life, what ye shall eat, or what ye shall drink; nor yet for your body, what ye shall put on. Is not the life more than meat, and the body than raiment? 26Behold the fowls of the air: for they sow not, neither do they reap, nor gather into barns; yet your heavenly Father feedeth them. Are ye not much better than they? 27Which of you by taking thought can add one cubit unto his stature. 28And why take ye thought for raiment? Consider the lilies of the field, how they grow; they toil not, neither do they spin: 29And yet I say unto you, That even Solomon in all his glory was not arrayed like one of these. 30Wherefore, if God so clothe the grass of the field, which today is, and tomorrow is cast into the oven, shall he not much more clothe you, O ye of little faith? 31Therefore take no thought, saying, what shall we eat? Alternatively, what shall we drink? Alternatively, Wherewithal shall we be clothed? 32(For after all these things do the Gentiles seek :) for your heavenly Father knoweth that ye have

need of all these things. [11] And when the Pharisees saw it, they said unto his disciples, Why eateth your Master with publicans and sinners?" (<u>Matthew 6:22-32</u>; <u>9:11</u>).

Learn how to lean on Him and look out for pressures from yourself and people around you. Do not do anything without the leading and support of God. Avoid any custom or tradition that opposes God's Word. Do not accept to marry anyone you do not like or love based on someone else's dreams, visions, prophecy or description. Insist on spiritual compatibility not only intellectual, monetary or physical compatibility. Be convinced that God is leading you before going to the altar for marriage vow and holy covenant. Seek God's kingdom first and you will get all that you would need in your marriage.

HOW GOD GUIDES HIS CHILDREN

Major decisions in life like marriage require divine guidance. Marital decision determines the direction one would follow in his life and may suggest how he may end his life both on earth and in eternity.

> *"Consider mine enemies; for they are many; and they hate me with cruel hatred"* (Psalms 25:19).

> *"And thine ears shall hear a word behind thee, saying, This is the way, walk ye in it, when ye turn to the right hand, and when ye turn to the left"* (Isaiah 30:21).

It is important therefore that believers surrender to God humbly for divine guidance. One who is guided by God will not experience sorrow or regret on earth. Wisdom guides believers to submit to God in order to enjoy His promise of guidance.

> *"Now it came to pass, as David sat in his house, that David said to Nathan the prophet, Lo, I dwell in an house of cedars, but the ark of the covenant of the LORD remained under curtains. Then Nathan said unto David, Do all that is in thine heart; for God is with thee. And it came to pass the same night, that the word of God came to Nathan, saying, Go and tell David my servant, Thus saith the LORD, Thou shall not build me an house to dwell in"* (1 Chronicles 17:1-4).

When you desire to hear from men instead of God, you would likely believe man rather than the Lord. God may not even bother talking to you if you have set your mind to get approval from men. You are to hear from God and confirm it through other means like men, not hear from man and force God to approve your marriage.

Likewise, you have to scrutinize your dreams and prove it repeatedly to know if God is involved how much more another person's dreams. This is because some dreams emanate from daily activities, thoughts, desires, intentions, imaginations and plans. However, few dreams come from God but you must be sure. It is wrong to seek advice from unserious ministers or backslidden prophets when you know that they no longer hear from God. When you are sure of your relationship with God, He would guide you and when He does, you will know.

> *"I will instruct thee and teach thee in the way which thou shall go: I will guide thee with mine eye"* (Psalms 32:8).

> *"The lines are fallen unto me in pleasant* places; *yea, I have a goodly heritage. I will bless the LORD, who hath given me counsel,: my reins also instruct me in the night seasons. I have set the LORD always before me: because* he is *at my right hand, I shall not be moved. Therefore, my heart is glad and my glory rejoices: my flesh shall rest in hope. For thou wilt not leave my soul in hell; neither wilt thou suffer thine Holy One to see corruption. Thou wilt shew me the path of life: in thy presence* is *fullness of joy; at thy right hand* there are *pleasures for evermore"* (Psalms 16:6-11).

God's guidance is a promise God would fulfill. Many believers believe in God's guidance and God guides such people. If you believe that God will guide you, He would and you will not regret it. God knows when you make Him number one in your life. When He proves that, He is happy to see you do His will to the end. When God is the one that leads you, His presence will never leave you as long as you stay with Him. It brings joy and peace to hand over the mantle of your marriage to God from the beginning until the end.

> *"To he the porter opened; and the sheep hear his voice: and he calleth his own sheep by name, and leaded them out. And when he putteth forth his own sheep, he goeth before them, and the sheep follow him: for they know his voice. And a stranger will they not follow, but will flee from him: for they know not the voice of strangers"* (John 10:3-5).

> *"I have yet many things to say unto you, but ye cannot bear them now. Howbeit when he, the Spirit of truth, is come, he will guide you into all truth: for he shall not speak of himself; but whatsoever he shall hear,* that *shall he speak: and he will shew you things to come"* (John 16:12-13).

> *"And I will pray the Father, and he shall give you another Comforter, that he may abide with you forever"* (John 14:16).

God sees our efforts to come to Him and He rewards them. He is able to open your ears to hear His voice. If He is the one leading you, He would carry you along. You cannot doubt God's presence if you are truly a child of God. He will reveal all things to you by His spirit.

> *"And he said, Go forth, and stand upon the mount before the LORD. And, behold, the LORD passed by, and a great and strong wind rent the*

mountains, and brake in pieces the rocks before the LORD; but *the LORD* was *not in the wind: and after the wind an earthquake;* but *the LORD* was *not in the earthquake: And after the earthquake a fire;* but *the LORD* was *not in the fire: and after the fire a still small voice"* (1 Kings 19:11-12).

"And the cherubim's were lifted up. This is *the living creature that I saw by the river of Chebar"* (Ezekiel 10:15).

"Father, glorify thy name. Then came there a voice from heaven, saying, *I have both glorified* it, *and will glorify* it *again. The people therefore, that stood by, and heard* it, *said that it thundered: others said, an angel spake to him. Jesus answered and said, This voice came not because of me, but for your sakes"* (John 12:28-30).

When you listen quietly, God will speak to you through His Spirit. This voice is of the indwelling Spirit of God. You can recognize voices of family members even when you are inside your room or bathroom. Likewise, if you belong to God's family, you would discern when your father or a stranger is speaking. This is true and natural. When a thief enters into your house, your little child can discern it is a stranger's voice even when he tries to pretend.

Everyone at home recognizes the voice of each member of the family. The only thing you need to do is to make sure you become a member of the family of God and learn the voices of each member. Until you can easily say, 'This is the one talking.' Jesus did not find it difficult to discern the voice of devil speaking through Peter and to know when God spoke through him also.

Believe it; you would hear God when He speaks unless you are not His child.

> *"And* though *the Lord give you the bread of adversity, and the water of affliction, yet shall not thy teachers be removed into a corner any more, but thine eyes shall see thy teachers: And thine ears shall hear a word behind thee, saying, This* is *the way, walk ye in it, when ye turn to the right hand, and when ye turn to the left"* (Isaiah 30:20-21).

Learn how to hear when God speaks henceforth. In that way, God can penetrate your heart and produce a deep conviction that cannot break easily. Do not wait until you are about to marry to start hearing from God. Sometimes, answers to your prayers could flash through your mind like a light or knowledge that comes suddenly and refuses to go even when you try to throw it off or forget it. At other times, thought or conviction can come slowly or gradually until they consume you.

> *"That the LORD called Samuel: and he answered, here* am *I. And he ran unto Eli, and said, Here* am *I; for thou calledst me. In addition, he said, I called not; lie down again. In addition, he went and lay down. And the LORD called yet again, Samuel. And Samuel arose and went to Eli, and said, Here* is *I; for thou didst call me. In addition, he answered, I called not, my son; lie down again. Now Samuel did not yet know the LORD neither was the word of the LORD yet revealed unto him. And the LORD called Samuel again the third time. And he arose and went to Eli, and said, Here* is *I; for thou didst call me. And Eli perceived that the LORD had called the child"* (1 Samuel 3:4-8).

24

> *"Afterward I came unto the house of Shemaiah the son of Delaiah the son of Mehetabeel, who was shut up; and he said, Let us meet together in the house of God, within the temple, and let us shut the doors of the temple: for they will come to slay thee; yea, in the night will they come to slay thee. And I said, Should such a man as I flee? In addition, who is there, that, being as I am, would go into the temple to save his life? I will not go in. And, lo, I perceived that God had not sent him; but that he pronounced this prophecy against me: for Tobiah and Sanballat had hired him"* (Nehemiah 6:10-12).

God has not changed the way He communicates with His people. He is still speaking today but the only thing is that many Christians are like Samuel at his youth, who could not discern the voice of God instantly. When God called him, he ran to Eli until he learnt how to hear and recognize God's voice. Eli knew it was God but Samuel did not know.

Nehemiah did not see God face to face, but the Word of God came to him. He perceived it was the Word of God and avoided evil and satanic traps. Such perception can come suddenly or gradually also but when it settles, you will know that this is the will of God. The Spirit of Christ helped him to know God's will.

> *"And immediately when Jesus perceived in his spirit that they so reasoned within themselves, he said unto them, why reason you these things in your hearts?"* (Mark 2:8).

> *"But he perceived their craftiness, and said unto them, why tempt you me?"* (Luke 20:23).

25

> *"And Jeremiah said, the word of the LORD came unto me, saying, Behold, Hanameel the son of Shallum thine uncle shall come unto thee, saying, Buy thee my field that is in Anathoth: for the right of redemption is thine to buy it. So Hanameel mine uncle's son came to me in the court of the prison according to the word of the LORD, and said unto me, Buy my field, I pray thee, that is in Anathoth, which is in the country of Benjamin: for the right of inheritance is thine, and the redemption is thine; buy it for thyself. Then I knew that this was the word of the LORD"* (Jeremiah 32:6-8).

Likewise, Jeremiah did not see God face to face but the Word of God came to him. Whenever the inspiration came, he spoke them out as he received them. The will of God may come to you as a strong impression and when it does, you will know.

> *"⁹Now when much time was spent, and when sailing was now dangerous, because the fast was now already past, Paul admonished* them, *¹⁰And said unto them, Sirs; I perceive that this voyage will be with hurt and much damage, not only of the lading and ship, but also of our lives. ¹¹ Nevertheless the centurion believed the master and ²¹But after long abstinence Paul stood forth in the midst of them, and said, Sirs, ye should have hearkened unto me, and not have loosed from Crete, and to have gained this harm and loss"* (Acts 27:9-11; 21).

As you start watching and listening to the voice of the Holy Ghost, you will be able to discover God's will for your marriage and other areas in your life.

"19While Peter thought on the vision, the Spirit said unto him, Behold, three men seek thee. 21Then Peter went down to the men which were sent unto him from Cornelius; and said, Behold, I am he whom ye seek: what is the cause wherefore ye are come?" (Acts 10:19; 21).

Sometimes you would ponder or doubt what the Lord has put in your heart or the vision you have received. That is when God sends another person to confirm it.

"Now there were in the church that was at Antioch certain prophets and teachers; as Barnabas, and Simeon that was called Niger, and Lucius of Cyrene, and Manaen, which had been brought up with Herod the tetrarch, and Saul. As they ministered to the Lord, and fasted, the Holy Ghost said, Separate me Barnabas and Saul for the work whereunto I have called them. And when they had fasted and prayed, and laid their hands on them, they sent them away" (Acts 13:1-3).

"Now when they had gone throughout Phrygia and the region of Galatia, and were forbidden of the Holy Ghost to preach the word in Asia, After they were come to Mysia, they assayed to go into Bithynia: but the Spirit suffered them not. And they passing by Mysia came down to Troas. And a vision appeared to Paul in the night; There stood a man of Macedonia, and prayed him, saying, Come over into Macedonia, and help us. And after he had seen the vision, immediately we endeavored to go into Macedonia, assuredly gathering that the Lord had called us for to preach the gospel unto them" (Acts 16:6-10).

God is able to send someone else to confirm what He has shown you in a vision or dream. God is not limited to lead in only one or two ways. The spirit of God can restrain you or caution you against carrying out a certain action or decision and then you find out that you are no longer willing or zealous to put that particular decision into action.

Sometimes, you may find yourself in confusion, sorrow, doubt, darkness or disturbance in your spirit because of a particular decision. At that point, you must wait and confirm God's will repeatedly before going further.

> *"¹⁴For God speaketh once, yea twice, yet man perceived it not. ¹⁵In a dream, in a vision of the night, when deep sleep falleth upon men, in slumbering upon the bed; ¹⁶Then he opened the ears of men, and sealed their instruction, ¹⁷That he may withdraw man from his purpose, and hide pride from man. ²³If there be a messenger with him, an interpreter, one among a thousand, to shew unto man his uprightness: ²⁴Then he is gracious unto him, and saith, Deliver him from going down to the pit: I have found a ransom"* (Job 33:14-17; 23-24).

> *"Set me as a seal upon thine heart, as a seal upon thine arm: for love is strong as death; jealousy is cruel as the grave: the coals thereof are coals of fire, which hath a most vehement flame. Many waters cannot quench love, neither can the floods drown it: if a man would give all the substance of his house for love, it would utterly be contemned"* (Songs of Solomon 8:6-7).

God is able to lead you also through direct revelation or divinely imparted love towards a particular person.

However, His revelation cannot contradict His will in any way. Likewise, God cannot tell or inspire you to marry a Delilah or Jezebel. If your love grows for Jezebel or Delilah, it cannot be the will of God. You cannot marry someone that worships idol and hope to convert her later. It is better to convert him or her first before thinking of marriage.

> *"Behold, I and the children whom the LORD hath given me* are *for signs and for wonders in Israel from the LORD of hosts, which dwelled in mount Zion. And when they shall say unto you, Seek unto them that have familiar spirits, and unto wizards that peep, and that mutter: should not a people seek unto their God? For the living to the dead?"* (<u>Isaiah 8:18-19</u>).

Your convictions about God must not differ. God cannot instruct you to marry an unbeliever who hates God and His children. We all know that God can lead someone through powerful divinely imparted love. This type of love can be bestowed upon the hearts of both couple supernaturally for each other and not one-sided. It is wrong for you to marry someone that does not love you. The love we are talking about is not temporal attraction, familiarity or self-induced love. We are talking about the supernatural love from God.

Do not marry someone because of beauty, material possession or position if you do not love him or her enough to live with him for better or worse. If you are about getting married and suddenly you lose your peace, spiritual joy and love, you have to stop for a rethink. You may need to seek God again. The troubling of spirit, sense of sorrow or lack of peace as if you have lost something valuable because of your decision may be a check and an indication that you are about to enter into bondage. Do not marry anyone

29

because you pity him or her. This is so dangerous and always counterproductive.

PRAYERS FOR A HAPPY MARRIED LIFE

Bible references: <u>Deuteronomy 7:1-4</u>; <u>Joshua 21:43-45</u>

Begin with praise and worship

1.   Any covenant that is fighting against God's will for my life, break, in the name of Jesus.

2.   Father Lord, lead me into Your perfect will for my marriage and keep me in it, in the name of Jesus.

3.   Let any power that is pushing me into satanic plans against God's plans be frustrated, in the name of Jesus.

4.   Blood of Jesus, speak me into Your perfect will for my marriage, in the name of Jesus.

5.   O Lord, lay the foundation of my marriage by Yourself, in the name of Jesus.

6.   I refuse to be manipulated into making a wrong choice, in the name of Jesus.

7.   I break and loose myself from any evil contact that was designed to take me away from God's will for my life, in the name of Jesus.

8.   Lord Jesus, deliver me from any evil relationship that is leading me into a wrong marriage, in the name of Jesus.

9.   O Lord, deliver me from the consequences of any covenant that I have ever broken, in the name of Jesus.

31

10. Let the curse and covenant of late marriage in my life break and expire, in the name of Jesus.

11. Every inherited evil covenant and curse in my life, I reject you, in the name of Jesus.

12. Anyone that is about to entice me into a wrong choice, I break away from you, in the name of Jesus.

13. I reject manipulation, bewitchment and spells that would lead me away from God's will for my life, in the name of Jesus.

14. Any wrong marriage that was arranged for me anywhere, I reject you, in the name of Jesus.

15. I break and loose myself from arrows of confusion in my choice of marriage partner, in the name of Jesus.

16. Any witch or wizard that has vowed to divert me from the will of God in marriage, fail, in the name of Jesus.

17. O Lord, anoint me to enter into a marriage that would strengthen faith, in the name of Jesus.

18. I command a perfect life partner to manifest and appear before me, in the name of Jesus.

19. I remove any power, thing or person that is blocking me from getting married to the right person, in the name of Jesus.

20. Let everything devil has put in place to deny me of God's perfect will in marriage be removed, in the name of Jesus.

21. Let the power of darkness that has vowed that I will not get married happily die, in the name of Jesus.

22. Father Lord, convince the perfect life partner to accept me fully and forever, in the name of Jesus.

23. O Lord, give me best partner that would help me to fulfill Your purpose, in the name of Jesus.

24. Let the marriage that would give me God's best in partnership, pleasures and fulfillment appear, in the name of Jesus.

25. Let that person that was ordained by God to fulfill my purpose of procreation, protection and provision appear, in the name of Jesus.

26. O Lord, use my life partner, whom I pray to meet, to preserve my purity, in the name of Jesus.

27. Father, lead me to a place where I can find the bone of my bone and the flesh of my flesh, in the name of Jesus.

28. Power that will bring my partner where I am, manifest and do so by force, in the name of Jesus.

29. O Lord, command my partner to accept me above any other, in the name of Jesus.

30. Lord Jesus, give me a life partner that would never expire or fade before my eyes, in the name of Jesus.

31. Let my life partner accept me above the way I do, in the name of Jesus.

32. O Lord, You know the best partner that is fit for me. Let him/her appear now, in the name of Jesus.

33. Powers that mislead others in the choices of marriage and are now fighting against me, die, in the name of Jesus.

34. Any power that is pulling my partner or me away, die, in the name of Jesus.

35. I disgrace any evil personality that wants to force me into a marriage that is against the will of God, in the name of Jesus.

36. O Lord, help me to succeed in every area of my life, in the name of Jesus.

37. Let intimidating power of God fall upon my partner and me to surrender to God's will, in the name of Jesus.

38. Let fake life partners that are coming my way fade away by force, in the name of Jesus.

39. Any evil garment that is covering my life partner or me, catch fire, burn to ashes, in the name of Jesus.

40. O Lord, I need You to lead me into the right marriage, in the name of Jesus.

41. Any marriage that was designed to ruin my destiny, I reject you, in the name of Jesus.

42. O Lord, replace my eyes with Yours that I may see Your will for my marriage, in the name of Jesus.

43. Father Lord, empower me to ignore and reject anything that was designed to mislead me, in the name of Jesus.

44. O Lord, be in-charge of my marriage from the beginning to the end, in the name of Jesus.

45. You, my will, plan and purpose, give way to God to rule and reign forever, in the name of Jesus.

46. O Lord, You are the best matchmaker, have Your way and link me to the best partner, in the name of Jesus.

47. I reject every marriage that was arranged by hell and I accept the one that was arranged by heaven, in the name of Jesus.

48. I reject demonic dreams, visions and prophecies from the devil, in the name of Jesus.

49. O Lord, give me a partner that will never cause me to regret my marriage, in the name of Jesus.

50. Blood of Jesus, speak my marriage out from the arrest of evil spirits, in the name of Jesus.

51. Let the marriage that will give me peace, rest and every good thing in life appear, in the name of Jesus.

52. Let the partner that will take me to divinely expected end manifest, in the name of Jesus.

53. Father Lord, let everything You have created do Your will, in the name of Jesus.

54. Father Lord, use every creature to confirm that You are leading me into this marriage, in the name of Jesus.

55. Let evil messengers in my marriage carry their messages to their senders, in the name of Jesus.

56. O Lord, make Your ways plain before my eyes, in the name of Jesus.

57. Let the light that would lead me to my life partner appear, in the name of Jesus.

58. Holy Spirit, minister to every enemy of my marriage to surrender and support me, in the name of Jesus.

59. Let the glory of my marriage appear, in the name of Jesus.

60. Let my choice of marriage partner be used to bless the world, in the name of Jesus.

Thank You So Much!

Beloved, I hope you enjoyed this book as much as I believe God has touched your heart today. I cannot thank you enough for your continued support for this prayer ministry.

I appreciate you so much for taking out time to read this wonderful prayer book, and if you have an extra second, I would love to hear what you think about this book.

Please, do share your testimonies with me by sending emails to pastor@prayermadueke.com, or through the social media at www.facebook.com/prayer.madueke. I invite you also to www.prayermadueke.com to view other books I have written on various issues of life, especially on marriage, family, sexual problems and money.

I will be delighted to partner with you in organized crusades, ceremonies, marriages and Marriage seminars, special events, church ministration and fellowship for the advancement of God's Kingdom here on earth.

Thank you again, and I wish you success in your life.

God bless you.

In Christ,

Prayer M. Madueke

OTHER BOOKS BY PRAYER M. MADUEKE

- *21/40 Nights Of Decrees And Your Enemies Will Surrender*
- *Confront And Conquer*
- *Tears in Prison*
- *35 Special Dangerous Decrees*
- *The Reality of Spirit Marriage*
- *Queen of Heaven*
- *Leviathan the Beast*
- *100 Days Prayer To Wake Up Your Lazarus*
- *Dangerous Decrees To Destroy Your Destroyers*
- *The spirit of Christmas*
- *More Kingdoms To Conquer*
- *Your Dream Directory*
- *The Sword Of New Testament Deliverance*
- *Alphabetic Battle For Unmerited Favors*
- *Alphabetic Character Deliverance*
- *Holiness*
- *The Witchcraft Of The Woman That Sits Upon Many Waters*
- *The Operations Of The Woman That Sits Upon Many Waters*
- *Powers To Pray Once And Receive Answers*
- *Prayer Riots To Overthrow Divorce*
- *Prayers To Get Married Happily*
- *Prayers To Keep Your Marriage Out of Troubles*
- *Prayers For Conception And Power To Retain*
- *Prayer Retreat – Prayers to Possess Your Year*
- *Prayers for Nation Building*
- *Organized student in a disorganized school*
- *Welcome to Campus*
- *Alone with God (10 series)*

CONTACTS

AFRICA
#1 Babatunde close,
Off Olaitan Street, Surulere
Lagos, Nigeria
+234 803 353 0599
pastor@prayermadueke.com

#Plot 1791, No. 3 Ijero Close,
Flat 2, Area 1,
Garki 1 - FCT, Abuja
+234 807 065 4159

IRELAND
Ps Emmanuel Oko
#84 Thornfield Square
Cloudalkin D22
Ireland
Tel: +353 872 820 909, +353 872 977 422
aghaoko2003@yahoo.com

EUROPE/SCHENGEN
Collins Kwame
#46 Felton Road
Barking
Essex IG11 7XZ GB
Tel: +44 208 507 8083, +44 787 703 2386, +44 780 703 6916
aghaoko2003@yahoo.com

Made in the USA
Coppell, TX
19 January 2022

71792210R00028